A Fine Dusting of

Brightness

Katie & Jim —
   Distance cannot separate true friends!
Thanks for you friendship.
                    Dorothy

© 2013 Dorothy Howe Brooks. All rights reserved. This material may not be reproduced in any form, published, reprinted, recorded, performed, broadcast, rewritten or redistributed without explicit permission of Dorothy Howe Brooks. All such actions are strictly prohibited by law.

ISBN-13: 978-0615839677

Cover: Collage, "Ritual Directions I," by Mary Derbes, photograph by Spencer Pullen.

Aldrich Press
24600 Mountain Avenue, Unit 35
Hemet, California 92544

In memory
James Johnston Howe, Jr.

Acknowledgements

The following poems previously appeared:

"On Touring The Battlefield At Little Round Top" in *The Village Writer*.
"Simple Fracture," in *RE: Arts and Letters (REAL)*.
"Alberta's Eyes," "Sunrise On Lake Lanier," "Elysian Fields," and "Doo-Wop Café" in *Georgia Journal*.
"Curved Space" in *Eclectic Journal*.
"Nocturne" in *The Louisville Review*.
"Photograph: Female Bather With Blonde Hair" in *Sojourner*.
"Weightless" and "The Father Wound" in *Community Journal*, DeKalb County, Georgia.
"Nude In Repose: Motel Room Off I-75," and "Pieta, 1998" in *Cumberland Poetry Review*.
"Shrödinger's Cat" in *Coe Review*.
"Half-Life" in *Chances Are . . ., A Chrysalis Reader*, Swedenborg Foundation.
"To My Mother, Growing Older," and "Cremation" in *Eureka Literary Magazine*.
"Black-Crowned Night Heron At The Peace River Wildlife Center" in *Iron Horse Literary Review*.
"Raphael: The Small Cowper Madonna" in *Carquinez Poetry Review*.
"Late Afternoon Nap, With Music" in *Louisiana Literature*.
"Magdalene" in *Windhover*, and in *National Catholic Reporter*.
"Blind" in *Poet Lore*.
"Silver Maples" in *Chaffin Journal*.
"Song of Songs" in *Schuylkill Valley Journal Of The Arts*.
"Elegy" in *California Quarterly*.
"Lost" in *Alembic*; also in <u>ArtPoems 2012</u> anthology.
"Annunciation" in *Front Range Review*.
"On A Moonless Night" in *River Oak Review*.
"In the Supermarket Line" in *Bayou*.

In addition, many of the poems previously appeared in the chapbook, <u>Simple Fracture</u>, published by New Spirit Press, or the chapbook, <u>Interstices</u>, published by Finishing Line Press.

Table of Contents

BEGINNER'S MIND 9

Section I

BIRDS ON A WIRE 13
LOST 15
ELEGY 16
VERMEER, *THE COOK* 17
NUDE IN REPOSE: MOTEL ROOM OFF I-75 18
PHOTOGRAPH: FEMALE BATHER WITH BLONDE HAIR, CONEY ISLAND, 1959 19
SONG OF SONGS 20
MAGDALENE 21
FOR JUST ONE NIGHT 22
SILVER MAPLES 23

Section II

ANNUNCIATION 27
WOMAN TENDING HER GARDEN 28
RAPHAEL: THE SMALL COWPER MADONNA 29
ALBERTA'S EYES 30
BLIND 31
CURVED SPACE 32
TO MY MOTHER, GROWING OLDER 33
ON A MOONLESS NIGHT 34

Section III

SIMPLE FRACTURE 37
ON TOURING THE BATTLEFIELD AT LITTLE ROUND TOP, GETTYSBURG, PENNSYLVANIA 39
WAR 40
HALF-LIFE 41
SCHRÖDINGER'S CAT 40
PIETA, 1998 46
THE FATHER WOUND 47
NOCTURNE 48
ELYSIAN FIELDS 50
DOO-WOP CAFE 51

Section IV

LOSING THE MAP	55
DIAGNOSIS	57
MY WAY	60
IN THE SUPERMARKET LINE	62
THE SLED	63
THINKING OF YOU	64

Section V

ALL THE LITTLE RITUALS	67
A FATHER'S LEGACY	68
WEIGHTLESS	69
CREMATION	71
FINAL GIFT	72
POWER FAILURE	74
PHOTOGRAPH—1945	75

Section VI

WE—A LOVE POEM	79
SUNRISE ON LAKE LANIER	80
LATE AFTERNOON NAP, WITH MUSIC	81
INTERSTICES	82
AFTER MAKING LOVE POEMS	83
BLACK-CROWNED NIGHT HERON	84
FRAGMENTS OF AUTUMN	85
AND STILLNESS COMES OVER THE LAND	87
AT THE EDGE OF THE LAND	88

ABOUT THE POET

BEGINNER'S MIND

A rift. Uncrossable.
The city below, unreachable,

like the past.
In the valley, clouds
drift,
obscure the land.

Here air
is pure, cloudless.

Awake now,
grateful,
I wonder
how it came to be,

this sudden
rising. This knowing.

Listening: as water
tumbles into meaning
like words.

Section I

BIRDS ON A WIRE

"reality takes shape in the memory alone"
M. Proust

This moment, this present
strung between past and future,

like the wire that is the perch
of hundreds of black birds—

starlings, far from their homes
in Canada or Michigan—

suspended
on this wire of the moment.

       *   *   *   *

Sometimes I wake in a strange hotel
the moment unhinged
from all the moments before and after,
a stark, bewildering clamor of the senses,
trying to discern in the half-light
windows and doors, what brought me here,
what journey, as the light
gradually fills the spaces,
and the furniture reappears:
desk, TV, faded chair, suitcases, and the past
returns the present to me.

       *   *   *   *

The past tethers me,
my grandmother said,

*without it I am afraid
I'd be adrift, an empty skiff
unmoored.*

        *   *   *   *

Without memory
I would be a waking dreamer:
like one blind from birth
suddenly given sight,
I'd see only
brilliant color patches
with no meaning.

        *   *   *   *

Yet, my grandmother—
during those last days,
as memory slowly unwound—
found herself

content. She welcomed each new day,
the marvel of sunlight on the wooden floor,
the lovely aroma of bacon frying,

her eyes
took in the strange new creation
unfolding before her
as her hands fluttered above the bedsheets
like birds.

LOST

He guides her into the church,
into the pew, one hand
loosely on her back, and she
lets him. She knows better
than to trust her tangled mind.
Amen, she says, and there's a moment
when it all falls into place
like shattered glass reassembling,
and she turns to him, her face
lights with recognition,
then all becomes wavery, sense
without substance.
She follows him
to the altar, tastes the bread,
the wine . . . for a moment
she stands—solitary,
uncertain, turns
toward the sound of voices
chanting from the rafters,
lifts her head, the light
from the stained glass
high above shatters
into brilliant blues and reds
on her shoulder and on
the marbled floor beneath:
she is lost there, waiting
for some sign, some sense,
she has slipped out of time
into this never-ending present,
like a child
who has wandered into a deep forest
filled with sounds
she can't name.

ELEGY

"the celebration of an element which absence has revealed."
  Eavan Boland

When I imagine my friend,
she is sitting with her husband
on their front porch steps,
it's Sunday, their anniversary,
a bright, summer day. Their son
comes up the walkway, holding a sympathy
card he bought for a classmate. *Oh,* they say,
joking, *a card for us,* and he, joking too,
drops it into their laps, like a small
explosive: *Happy Anniversary.*
Then he's off, late to meet friends,
spend the day on their boat.

It's evening when I arrive:
she's in the back bedroom, door shut,
he's in his chair, staring dry-eyed,
their grief a white-hot presence
no one dare touch. The neighbors crowd in,
bringing food. *They've dragged the lake*,
they say, *they've found the body. Imagine,
only nineteen, . . .* But I prefer to imagine
them back into that morning,
the sun on their faces, the dishes done,
the whole day ahead of them,

innocent, and as yet unaware
of their happiness.

VERMEER, *THE COOK*

oil on canvas, circa 1658

Like a fine dusting
of brightness, the light settles
on everything it touches:
the pitcher, the stream of milk,
forehead of the woman, even
the folds of her gown
and folds of cloth on the table.

Say the light *enters* the room,
that it *streams* in the window
as if a shimmering rain
of particles, but that's not
how Vermeer paints it. The light
is merely there, a glow
as if from within—her skin
luminous, the loaf of bread shining—

Yet somehow the light remains
separate from the objects:
transient, and insubstantial.
Vermeer's light is ephemeral.
*Imagine this scene
without light*, Vermeer
seems to say. *And hold instead
this ordinary moment: This life.*

NUDE IN REPOSE: MOTEL ROOM OFF I-75

In the dark she can't see
the walls hung with tawdry art,
the worn carpet, only his body,
breath steady and deep,
his head on one arm, stomach flaccid,
penis now slack against the tangled sheets,
his back a single line
shoulder to waist to hip to thigh,
a perfect contour that she traces
with her fingertips. The light from the window,
cool white of the halogen streetlamps,
plays on his fine skin
like moonlight on marble.
She imagines Adonis not dead
but asleep by a stream,
Aphrodite gazing upon him,
wildflowers covering his head, his hands.
Why not? Why not gaze upon this body,
this perfect line and desire it,
the flesh cold like marble? A warrior fallen,
a god asleep in the meadow. Why not
kingdoms to possess this body?
If she were a sculptor, she would
shape this perfect form from stone,
mold the rounded torso, smooth the skin,
if she were a painter, she would dip her brush
into the ink and trace the line,
the single perfect line that re-creates the body,
she would set the light from the window,
cool and pale, to glint off the curved shapes
like moonlight, sharp white outline
against the midnight blackness,
pure line, pure form.

PHOTOGRAPH: FEMALE BATHER WITH BLONDE HAIR, CONEY ISLAND, 1959

Her perfectly perm'ed head is still
above water, but she's getting in deeper.
She comes every day. She's been coming
a long time. She wades in the shallows,
looks out to sea, searches the horizon
as if she sees something, or desires
something too far out for her to grasp.
The sky is blank, the water calm:
no answers there. Someone,
her mother perhaps, told her
a coiffed head and a single strand of pearls
would see her through anything.
She hadn't counted on an ocean.
I can feel her longing.
She wants to go deeper, the water
to wash over her face, cool her forehead, but
she's afraid. When she dives down
(as I'm sure she will) she'll emerge
different—hair straight and stiff, mascara
(for I'm certain she wears it)
streaking her cheeks like black tears.
Already she can feel the sandy bottom
begin to give way.
She's going to have to go under.
She's going to have to learn to swim.
Even her pearls won't save her.

SONG OF SONGS

The mockingbird sings a song
not her own, yet

you know her voice.
You know it the way

you know your child's cry,
the way she calls to you

from the swing set, or her room late at night,
the way you finally

know your own voice
in spite of the clever imitations

you've practiced for so long.
Some evening alone in the quiet

words begin to take shape,
a first faint whisper, then a melody,

then at last you hear the song,
the one song that is yours,

and in your own voice
sing back. O Mockingbird!

MAGDALENE

"They have taken my Lord away and I don't know where they have put Him."
Jn 20:13

This was a matter for the men.
But I could never keep silent
any more than I could calm
my unruly hair, though both marked me.
Bold, I went where my heart led.
But I was still tight in a bud, still trying
to be the quiet, self-less woman
who knew her place, still ashamed.
Until I turned—
              "Mary," he said,
and my heart answered.
He knew me better than I knew
myself: "Go, tell the others,"
he said, "bear the good news . . ."
and I blossomed.

FOR JUST ONE NIGHT

If only we could, for just one night,
wear our jeans skin-tight and a loose silky blouse
with no bra, brush our hair, long, till it shines
on our shoulders, curves over one eye,
flirt like mad with those dark, male bodies
that lined every corner of our youth,
sly-eyed. If only we could open ourselves
to them in some dim motel, or parked car
without fear, or love, without regret,
be—for one night—skin and tongue
and warm, moist enclosures
and nothing more. If only our mothers
could say to us, live, taste life, be
women, while we were still new
and unformed, while desire was still
a sharp, anonymous pain in our loins.

SILVER MAPLES

      The landscapers have come.
They swarm over the six maples
like ants who find a half-eaten sandwich,
pull it apart crumb by crumb and bear it away.
The sound of the chainsaw cuts the morning
birdsong, a long loud whrrrum, a crash,
then silence, before the engine revs up again,
whrrrrum.
               They call these maples
silver—silver is the color
of the flimsy blossoms the tree buds with in spring,
frail lacy pods that drip from each tiny branch
like hundreds of butterfly cocoons, but smaller and empty,
or baby's breath scattered through a bride's bouquet:
no one notices it among the brilliant gardenias,
the lilies of the valley trailing down, no one is supposed to,
but it plays off the white petals like a faint halo.
The trees are a perfect shape, round and full,
a child's drawing of a tree, and for two days
this spring covered in silver
they were like full-sized replicas
of a woman's charm bracelet,
                          but that's not why
they're called silver. No, in summer the breeze
lifts the leaves to reveal an underside
finished with a dusky glaze like a wax
someone forgot to buff, or a mirror
gone crazed with age. The leaves are light
and move easily in the air, and the veins
of their backsides shimmer like the soft silver webbing
of a spider. Silver Maples.
                             But their roots
crawl underground like veins of silver

winding their way through stone, soft and elemental:
a hidden stream, water slithering through rock,
eating a path to the surface. They soak up water
from nearby grass, plants, shrubs, leave them
dry and defenseless, reach into foundations,
crack sidewalks and driveways, split houses apart,
under the ground these trees are more like kudzu, tough
and tenacious, they'll destroy a lawn
faster than crabgrass or dandelions,
                                                    but now
the trees are covered with green-suited men, workmen
from another state with ropes and harnesses,
who never saw the trees in spring, or even in fall
when the red begins at the outer tips and spreads
like a stain across the whole tree, these men
are paid to do a job, and they collect the severed limbs
and haul them away in a truck until only naked trunks
remain and those they chop away, too, and the stumps
they bulldoze, even the roots they tear out, break up
and drag away . . .
                            Now there's no sign
of maples. The yard neatly covered in sod,
row upon row, misses nothing.
Sidewalks lie flat and unmoving.
The foundation is safe. The house
has no memory. Spring comes
and fall. Children play in the yard,
cars drive by. Grass grows easily.
The bright sun bears down,
remembers nothing.

Section II

ANNUNCIATION

Of all the inhabitants of this church,
she's the one tendered for our existence,
the one, head bowed, acquiescing.

A girl, too soon a mother, she's caught up
in history. In the story we tell
she is visited by an angel

gives her assent, her small life.

For this, we mold her in plaster of Paris,
dress her in blue like the sky,
paint her eyes downcast,

place her heel on the serpent's fang.
We call her *mother,* we call her
virgin: impossibly pure, impossibly

good. Young girls crown her
with roses each May, believe
her impossible surrender.

They worship at her altar.

WOMAN TENDING HER GARDEN

The woman bends
to the Kabocha plant,
gently dips her finger
deep into the male flower,
gathers the pollen dust,
and places it ever so carefully
into the female. Fruit
will come of this,
a green pumpkin like the one
near the ground,
large, and not yet ripe.
She kneels, feels
its rough skin, its round
firmness. She knows
about ripeness, about waiting.
She places both hands
on her swollen belly,
then rises, lifts
her hand to block the sun.
These long, hot
afternoons: Summer
is slowly turning to Fall.
The pumpkin ripens
in its own time.

RAPHAEL: THE SMALL COWPER MADONNA

It's the way she holds him
Loosely, like she's tired
And he has become a burden
Though he weighs nothing
And is already turning away.

Almost a child herself,
Her eyes fix on something
Just beyond the infant's shoulder,
While he's alert,
About to climb down from her lap:

That first step, the tiny hand
Slipping from her neck.
Her whole body sags in response,
One long sigh. Behind her,
Mountains, a lake, the temple,

All of no consequence,
For she is forever centered here:
A womb, a breast, a lap,
A supporting hand
Ever beginning to let go.

ALBERTA'S EYES

My mother is shrinking.
Her bones grow shorter as I
grow taller. She is collapsing
in on herself like a white
dwarf. I imagine

standing beside her
as she disappears into me,
a spent genie returning
to its home, her hair a silver
wisp of smoke trailing behind.

Friends say, *You have Alberta's
eyes.* They find her,
young again, in my gestures,
the tilt of my head, places
I'd never think to look.

BLIND

My mother recalls a poem on blindness
written by a friend
when both were eighteen.
Now, the friend long dead, my mother
reaches for those words
to say the things she can't yet say,
to name her loss:
the poplar outside the window,
velvet-hearted pansies,
favorite books,
lamplight.

"How did she know?" my mother asks,
"We were so young, and *blind*
was no more
than a sentimental idea,
something we read about in poems."

CURVED SPACE

Emptiness unfurls the boundless night,
                            curls around flaming stars
        circles the planets
               like a mother
          enfolding her young,
                    holding them dear
    as they hurl through time,

keeping them safe

      keeping them bound,
                        each star
                              each swirling galaxy
              a jeweled moment
                    in the life of the universe,

sacred web, weaving eternity into being.

TO MY MOTHER, GROWING OLDER

At times you *are* loss, and not the memory of it.
You carry it in your bearing, and so
I stay away too long. I fear the knowledge you bring:
That senses die first, one by one, and with them
Birdsong, the colors of dawn, faces of our children.
That each day brings a new grief: today,
The death of a friend. Death is a word
You no longer fear.
                              When I leave you
I buy bulbs to plant in my garden,
Hold my children close, memorize faces.
Outside, I kneel in the fresh dirt. I dig furiously.

ON A MOONLESS NIGHT

like this—the air so clear it disappears—
the sky rises like a vast mountain,
all those stars, bits of silvery rock
come to rest on its side. The Dipper
brought me out this evening,

it hovered outside my window
like a secret, and I had to rise
and go. Outside, the stars gathered
in the patterns I knew from childhood:
brave Orion, Cassiopeia in her chair,

the Pleiades, all the names and stories
you taught me so long ago. Nothing
had changed, the way, here,
since you've gone,
everything has changed.

In the blackness, the space between,
I imagine I can see
time, limitless time, all the way
back to that first bang, a connection
to all the ages past, and to you—

on a night like this, I remember
when I first moved to the sea,
when age had dimmed your sight,
you said, your voice soft with longing,
"The stars must be so bright there."

Section III

SIMPLE FRACTURE

I held his hand—
a simple thing.
I would have knitted
his whole arm back together
if I could.

His hand held mine
tight, tighter, squeezing
as the surgeon prepared
to snap the broken bone
back into place.

I watched his face,
red, contorted, crying out
in pain, squeezed hard
like the nurse's arm
on my stomach squeezing
out the child: breathe,
breathe deeply, cry, cry out
the pain, first the head, breathe,
then the body, cry out, this same
body now holding on tight,
tighter, this same child, boy, man-
child squeezing me, holding me
tight against the pain.

Then it was over.
He rested against my body
like the infant I first
held tight.

But all the while,
all the time his hand held mine,
my eyes, unflinching, held his
the way the center holds,
the way love carries us through.

ON TOURING THE BATTLEFIELD AT LITTLE ROUND TOP, GETTYSBURG, PENNSYLVANIA

We stand together, you and I, yet you see
there on the stretches of grass
armies assembled, brigades engaged
in flanking maneuvers, generals
vying for control of the high ground,
strategic positions marked off
by stone breastworks, rows of cannons.

I see a barren Wheatfield
littered with muskets, blackened
remains of yesterday's campfires,
saplings trampled, a blanket wasted,
an unmatched shoe, broken horses,
sons who will be missing from all
the family celebrations to come.

Up the hill to Little Round Top—
acting out the heritage of centuries
of volunteers who took up arms,
with trembling valor, to defend flags
and mothers back home—
armed with the memory of a young
Meade or Lee, our sons

scamper in play. Mock epaulets pinned
to small shoulders, toy weapons aimed
at a brother's heart.

We stand together, you and I.

WAR

I am more afraid of war
than death. If war came
I would take my sons
and stuff them in the bottom of the clothes hamper,
sit on top, smiling,
I have no sons, I would say,
smothering them as I spoke.
I would gather them under my skirts,
face alone the machine-gun fire,
bare-chested, bullets dancing from my breasts.
I have no sons.
I won't allow you
to talk of glory and sacrifice. I won't
hear of history and causes.
My sons are golden,
young men on the brink. They believe
the stories. But I know better. Like Kronos,
I'd devour them, one by one, ingest them
back into this body, this womb.
They are my flesh, and while I live
no war will take my sons.

HALF-LIFE

I.

That invisible spark,
bundle of radiant energy
released as one atom transforms,
laser-sharp, brilliant
as a shooting star
then gone.
Chance selection, yet
one atom's decay
preserves the rest.

II.

Boys will defy—
they hang from pitons,
dive into murky water,
trespass on footbridges—
they dare their immortal bodies
to fail them.

We can't save them all.
One or two slip,
their bodies radiating
all that youthful energy
in one splendid burst,
burnt offering
to the god of fickle chance.

We can't save them. Yet they,
by their going, save us.

SCHRÖDINGER'S CAT

> *"For the observer, there can only be two outcomes: the cat is alive or dead. But in the quantum world, the many possible solutions exist simultaneously."*
> <u>Looking Glass Universe</u>

A cat in a box. Imaginary cat,
hypothetical box. Probable?

Schrödinger's cat had kittens.
They lost their mittens.

No, no. Schrödinger's cat.
In the box. Electrons firing.

Is the cat alive? Half
alive? Half dead? Open the box.

The gingham dog and the calico cat.
They ate each other up. No? No.

Schrödinger's cat in the box.
Dead.

      *   *   *   *

When George drowned
we were sailing
on that very same lake
we saw the Coast Guard
the rescue boats
heard the sirens

we trimmed our sails
tacked away
later much later
when night was falling
deep and heavy
the wind had dropped
we were full
calm like the water
we docked our boat
folded the sails
sang lullabies
climbed into the car
headed toward that knowing.

George lived for us
a whole day longer.

        *   *   *   *

Pussy cat, pussy cat, where have you been?
I've been up to London to visit the queen.

Reality, that Schrödinger wave
of probability, collapses

when he opens the box:
the momentary meeting

of space and time.
Schrödinger's cat: Dead.

Because he looked.

*   *   *   *

A messenger, before the days of telephones,
rides on horseback, alone, fast,
a two-day journey, cradling his knowledge:
his brother, slain for him, but still alive—
Mother mending her boy's jacket, Father
stoking the fire, listening for his sons—
galloping, galloping, the horse sweating,
carrying that word, that story
that will kill his brother again.

*   *   *   *

Imagine an information network
faster than telephones.

Imagine peering into the box,
always seeing the cat, always knowing.

Imagine certainty.

*And all the king's horses
and all the king's men . . .*

*   *   *   *

We parked the car
opened the door

switched on the light
unloaded the sailing gear
the telephone
was ringing
full of its news

the messenger
galloping
the cat in the box
long dead.

PIETA, 1998

In some emergency room this morning
a mother held her son's limp body,
felt for a pulse, shouted, "I love you,
wake up," and, "Why did you do this, why?"

and after four hours the boy finally woke
with no answers, nothing for his mother
except his lean sixteen-year-old body
alive, face turned toward the wall.

Next week they'll try to forget this morning,
let the rush of ordinary mornings—
brushing teeth, pouring juice—seal the memory
with scar tissue, thick and unyielding.

It wasn't my son. I wasn't that mother.
And if I were, would I be telling this story?
Or would I know, as she must know,
that stories are easy, imagination cheap:

they can't touch the truth
of a woman
alone
in a hospital
holding her child.

THE FATHER WOUND

The story of Abraham sacrificing his son
was given to me as a story of faith.
Abraham believed. Even as he led Isaac
up the mountain, noticed the way the light
dazzled his son's curls, the lean strength
of his legs, cool green of his eyes, still
he believed: "God will provide."
Later I saw it as a story of trust:
Abraham giving his child back to God.

But now I have a son. Tall,
smooth-skinned. And I think of Isaac:
A son who sees his father
raise the knife over his bare chest
knows he is alone. That knife cut
the bond between father and son,
freed Isaac from his father's long shadow.
Never again could he look up
to his father as if he were god.
They walked down the mountain,
separate. I imagine they were silent.
The rest of his life, when others called him
son of Abraham, son of the prophet,
the boy would see the steel blade
poised above his throat.

NOCTURNE

*Who will bring back to me the months that have gone
And the days when God was my guardian . . .*
        Job 29;2

I keep seeing his face,
polite, half-smile, shoulders hunched slightly,
an attitude of respect but never without dignity,
hoarding his dignity: not a man to be pitied.
He's watching his daughter, the eldest,
as she steps forward into the light,
large-rimmed glasses, straight shoulder-length hair,
hint of a giggle as embarrassed, yet proud, too,
she seats herself at the piano, raises the bench—
she's small like her father, a good six inches
shorter than the boy before her, she winds the knobs
with both hands and slowly rises. Now
she's ready. Again the smile, she takes a breath,
straightens the sheet music—on the sofa
her brother and sister squirm, her mother
full of serenity, waits—and she begins:
a Chopin nocturne, her fingers gracing the keys,
the music flowing like a river from her native China,
like the crane in ancient paintings
bearing strength, harmony, intricate as calligraphy,
it touches each of us in that room,
the mother on the sofa, the brother and sister,
now still, the other kids, nervous, waiting their turn,
the father in the back row, standing,
hands crossed before him. I see his face
as he watches her, head nodding. He's heard her
play this piece over and over, no doubt,
getting the notes right, the timing perfect,
perhaps he's listened as he lay awake nights
the way I hear my son, late, in the dark,
the music seeping through the walls, winding

up the staircase, night music; he is a man
not to be pitied, yet—
                              I keep seeing his face—

I imagine it

as the news reports trickle in:
         airplane,
                  wreckage,
                            no survivors . . .
He's at his safe desk,
         but his family . . .
                  on vacation . . .
his wife, his son, his two girls,
                  on the plane . . .

this plane.

He is a quiet man, a solitary man,
whose daughter once played Chopin,
who clapped politely as she rose and bowed,
always believing he would hear her play again.

                         For Lynda

ELYSIAN FIELDS

Slippery, silver light washed the beach
stark white, formed sharp shadows
of sea oats and abandoned castles,
sparked the edges of waves slipping ashore.

A night in bold relief: dark figures,
glowing earth, black sky. My sons,
two gilt-edged silhouettes,
frolicked like ghost stallions, daring

the moon's light to capture them.
They were mortals, stumbled upon the gods'
playground, and I was afraid for them, afraid
they might slip through the edge of darkness,

afraid Diana would hunt them for sport,
or Neptune rise from the sea to claim them.

DOO-WOP CAFE

*"And Peter said, 'Master, it is good for us
to be here. Let us set up . . . tents. . .'"*
      (Mark 9:5)

The ordinary night falls around us,
blots out strip malls, fast food restaurants.
They drop behind like forgotten toys.
Our narrow headlights reach into the next moment,
pull us along, while the radio sings out memories:
Doo-Wop Café—Fabulous Fifties and Sixties.

In the back seat our kids, slipping headlong
into adolescence, grab hold, pick up the beat:
*Breaking Up Is Hard To Do. Yakety Yak.
Goin' Out of My Head.* We whirl
through the blackness past fields of Georgia clay
like time travelers, windows sealed against the heat,
the future. Our songs. We rocked them to sleep
to these: *Good Vibrations. It's So Easy.*
Laughter, shrieks, as they lean into the curves,
into the rhythms, into each other.

If I could, I'd travel this midnight road
all the way to New York . . .
        I'd keep the darkness . . .
                I'd build us a tent . . .

Section IV

LOSING THE MAP

A map is not the thing itself.
        Inside the brain is a map.
Roads and streams on the map really exist.
But not on the map.
    The map in the brain is made of cells and neurons.
    The cells and neurons create a picture in the brain.
The map is a picture of the land.
It is a metaphor of the land.
Or not.
      It is not the thing itself, not the streets
     and buildings and houses, but an image of the thing.
An explorer has no map.
An explorer has to create the map.
       The brain makes its own map.
      Over days and weeks it creates the map.
It takes many weeks to record all the features
that become the map.
     The map inside the brain tells us where we are,
       and how to get downtown,
    how to get to the kitchen, to the bedroom.
Lewis and Clark had no map.
        The brain can lose its map.
     When the brain loses its map,
      it becomes an explorer with no map.
They found their way across the country.
They created the map.
     Without a map there is nothing to follow.
They followed the rivers.
     No rivers in the brain to follow.

Without a map, everything was strange.
Everything was new.
Everything is strange.
Everything is new.
Lewis and Clark made the map.
They found their way home.
The brain tries, every day, to recreate the map.
But can't
It is lost. Like you. It can't find its way.

DIAGNOSIS

I.

Begin with what you know:
Trees outside the window
stark, leafless,
the sun's light weak.
The birds are gone.
But this is not death:
death has no Spring.

II.

Begin with what you know:
A memory—you and I
on the beach at dusk,
you the round-faced boy laughing,
running, the kite soaring above,
me the skinny big sister beside you,
"Hold on, hold on . . ."

the way I say to you now,
Hold on.

III.

You remember it differently:
the boy trips, he drops the string,
the sister is crying, the kite
falls into the sea.

IV.

When you are gone,
pieces of my oldest stories
will be forever
missing.

V.

Begin again:
The butterfly lives a week,
the sea turtle a century:
everything dies.

This is what we know, but to live
we pretend
not to know.

VI.

Where to begin?
A late night phone call,
images on a scan,
that thing inside your head
alien, mysterious,
alive—

consuming you from within.

VII.

Begin again, and again,
and again,
each beginning

leads back to you
bereft.
Yet even the stars die out, one by one.
Even the sun.

MY WAY

All day at the hospital again—
we argued—more chemo,

hospice, how to help your wife,
who should have power

of attorney, you stubborn
as always, still not resigned,

still fighting. Now
the cheap hotel bar, Sinatra

impersonator, another glass
of wine, and how good it feels

to be alone.
The room empties out, darkens,

candles cast soft shadows,
the day drains away. The singer

moves near, cups the microphone
with both of his hands,

lowers his eyes, croons, *And now
the end is come* . . . the room,

the candles, the glass of wine,
all disappear into blackness:

He is singing just to me.
His words are leading me

into a dark and sacred place,
a place I am afraid to enter.

IN THE SUPERMARKET LINE

In the bright fluorescence,
it seemed a blazing light shone
on cashiers, customers, bag boys alike.
The counters glowed. Outside
the day was too soon giving way
to darkness. I was encased
in thick glass: though lips moved,
no sound penetrated. The woman
scanned the bread, the milk,
she wore a tag that said *Betty Ann*,
and a black hair net. I watched
myself as if from a great distance
hand her a bill, pocket the change.
Behind the checkout stand
packets of razor blades, sugarless gum,
stood in neat rows,
like messages from a far-off land.
I walked unsteadily towards the door,
felt the ground tilt and sway.
Here I was, in this ordinary place,
so lately come from your bedside,
the long vigil ended.
I hadn't realized how the earth
had shifted on its axis, how everything—
even light—was out of balance.

THE SLED

Even at half-price, I mocked you
for wasting your money,
our one southern snowfall
already weeks past. But days later,
the snow returned, the schools closed.
"Is my sled still under my bed?"
you asked, your voice weak,
a sore throat keeping you in bed.
And I reassured you, until the snow
piled so high on the hills behind our house
that I could no longer resist. All afternoon
on your new sled, I glided down
those snowy hillsides, the cold wind
in my face, that sensation of raw speed
a new and welcome thrill: grateful,
as if you had willed this just for me.

So it is now, with you gone, I greet
each new day like a rare snowfall:
Look! The sun is shining!
The hills are covered in white!
The empty sled is waiting.

THINKING OF YOU

Already I'm looking back
on your last year.
How quickly time
has done its winnowing,
removed all traces
of midnight phone calls,
piles of insurance forms,
that absent-minded doctor
who couldn't even
remember your name;
but preserved your jokes
about losing your way
to the bathroom and
discovering your left hand
again and again.

One whole year
we squandered: you
going from doctor to doctor,
me across the country
saying I would visit
next week, *next* month, *next* . . .

We spent our days
like the man who hands over
his last dollar for a lottery ticket,

or the woman whose young son
is waving good-bye from the school bus,
but she, in her hurry, fails to notice.

Section V

ALL THE LITTLE RITUALS

Each evening, from the wooden pipestand
he had carved himself, my father chose a pipe—
curved ivory with a deep bowl,
or sleek, black-stemmed trimmed in silver—
then slowly filled it with tobacco.
He tamped it down with his thumb
to just the right density, then,
striking the match, applied the flame,
puffing in and out, little puffs of smoke
rising to the ceiling. The fragrance
hung in the air. He held the bowl
in his left hand and talked as he smoked,
filling our young heads with the marvels
of science: light-years and black holes,
the ever-expanding universe.
We'd question, he'd pause,
again, the match, again the flame,
as the sweet smoke circled our heads
and the evening faded to dusk.
And when night came, the room
grown still, the tobacco reduced to ash,
these strange and wonderful
ideas sparked to life in us
as intangible as distant shooting stars.
He emptied the remains into the ashtray,
careful not to spill the tiny embers
that still glowed in the growing dark.
"That's what I like about a pipe,"
he would say, "all the little rituals."

A FATHER'S LEGACY

Long afternoon shadows fingered our toy car
as we followed the steep asphalt corridor
through the ripe October day.

Painted leaves clung to familiar branches
for yet another hour, playing out
anew Nature's ancient ritual.

I honored your sad, stoic silence
as you steered us to our destination.

In the small, downstairs room the old man
slept, a single light near his bed
holding back the coming darkness.

You lifted his head, caressing it
with a gentleness I had forgotten.
You cradled his frail body, supporting him.

I saw the tears form in your eyes
and a softness come into your face
that I knew and remembered.

We kept our vigil
while outside the dying sun set the mountains aflame.
It was ourselves we tended.

WEIGHTLESS

I hold you now.
You are dead

weight my hands can mold
into the shape I need:

stern father,
father forgiving.

I gather up your flannel shirts
worn thin,

your tired trousers,
raise the cardboard box

buried beneath your underwear,
spill out

private pieces of you,
reassemble them, seal them away.

Your cane behind the door
insisting: *I lived once,*

I lived—

my fingers grasp
its cold rough wood,

afraid to let go of it, afraid
of the dizzying drop,

that first weightless moment . . .
when I open wide my hands

you've slipped away.

CREMATION

shall we gather
        beside the fire
                as at the grave
light the flame

pile your worn coat
            your cane
                  atop the pyre
          sing hymns

touch your cold fingers
            one last time
                  your naked feet

will we smell the burning flesh
       feel heat

what memory shall we have
            what marble marker
                      what place
upon this whole earth to seek you out

                and will the flames
     the sweet flames
          hold your body
              like a lover

     speak your name

FINAL GIFT

One day too soon
student doctors will gather
as around a banquet table,

nervous, expectant, joking
away the tensions. The balding
professor, wise but distant,

will strip back the sheet
covering your body.
His cold scalpel

will carve you open,
expose you
to those clever eyes:

your enlarged heart, worn
arteries, even your fluid-
filled lungs, so desperately

wrung for one last breath,
that finally collapsed
bringing you here, reduced

to nothing more
than faded flesh,
brittle bone. Bit by bit

they will take you apart,
examine each organ,
memorize tissue, muscle,

they will consume you
like carrion
and you will live

in their learning.
After they have taken their fill,
after what remains

is returned to dusty ashes,
a part of you, a part
we didn't even know

existed, will endure.
In their healing, you
will find immortal life.

POWER FAILURE

All afternoon with no TV, we watched
ice form on the pines,
heard the limbs crack and break,
as the house grew gradually colder,
the car abandoned on the icy street,
microwave impotent. When we opened
the refrigerator, no light greeted us,
and we had to search for milk and cheese,
make cold sandwiches for supper. We sat
in the growing dark and talked quietly
so as not to disturb the quiet, finally,
late, we climbed into bed and clung
to each other for warmth—

the way we did the night you died,
when everything was suddenly
different.

PHOTOGRAPH—1945

Close-up: a woman swings her child
high above her head. The mother,
young, handsome, hair blown back,
sunlight on her face, laughs
for her baby, the child, curly-
haired, serious, looks away—
toward the strange man crouched
behind the lens. (The man no doubt
still wears his Navy Lieutenant's
uniform. I imagine him
studying his new-found daughter
through the camera's sharp eye.)

Just a mother and a baby, nothing
more—no banners, no victory parade—
only a woman, and a child
raised to the sky in celebration.

Section VI

WE—A LOVE POEM

You are the *we* of all my poems.
You are the hand I reach for in the dark,
the sound of evening rain,
the music to my words,
and the silences between.
You are my mooring, my compass,
the wind in my hair.
You are the other, the argument
and the make-up after.
You are not the sun or the moon,
but a tiny light, never extinguished:
an ember, a struck match,
a firefly at dusk.
You are the buoy marking safe harbor:
you are the harbor. I rest there.
You are the subject of this poem,
and the object of all my imaginings:
You are the first person plural of me.

SUNRISE ON LAKE LANIER

In the cooling, in the green, the deep,
a breath, a whisper of light breaks,
spills into dark folds of night,
splashes on tiny waves, fingers
caressing the hull relentless
as a lover, thick water holding us,
lifting us, slow thick speech,
night nestled in your eyes,
in mine, stiff limbs of tangled
sleep. No sun, only wet fog,
heavy, dew-laden rosy silence
like lake rising to meet sky.

LATE AFTERNOON NAP, WITH MUSIC

Your skin tastes of Ivory,
        its fragrance
the fresh-washed scent of baby's fine hair.

The room darkens, gradually
        empties itself
of the spent day. On the stereo

a Beethoven sonata, the notes a literal
        presence, something
we hold on to as we drift

toward sleep. Later, much later,
        night upon us
we wake to silence.

INTERSTICES

I long for words
but words are not your friend;
instead, you speak to me
in silences: a look, a gesture,
a touch, a presence. The body
has a language
all its own, cannot lie,
speaks always in the present tense
yet carries our whole shared history.
Truer than words:
the interstices of conversation,
the space between.
I am learning your ways.

AFTER MAKING LOVE POEMS

After the empty page is filled
       the sweaty concentration breaks
              the vision like two bodies colliding dims
                     after the pulsing rhythm subsides

I say the words out loud
       savor each one like blackberries
              gathered on a thorny hillside
                     above the interstate's pressing heat

succulent fruit ripe for harvest
       the sudden sticky sweetness
             spilling from our lips turning
                     the afternoon into a love ballad

verses rolling off my tongue
       their taste damp and bittersweet
             as your breath in my tangled hair
                     your naked body curving into mine—
satisfied.

BLACK-CROWNED NIGHT HERON
AT THE PEACE RIVER WILDLIFE CENTER

He's mad with nest-building.

He can't help himself. Something
with an urgency like hunger
tells him: if he builds it well
she will come,

a mate, her head crowned
with three fine feathers like his,
rare plumes others have died for.

So all day
he scavenges the cage floor,
collects sticks and branches,
weaves them into a nest,

and each evening tears it up again.

She will never come,

though he's diligent as a schoolboy
and handsome as any bird here.

FRAGMENTS OF AUTUMN

I.

The river today
like glazed steel
reflecting in perfect symmetry
mud banks, trees, even
the cloudless sky.
How can we know
when sight betrays us
which is real, which illusion?

II.

My eyes are blind
as the fog-shrouded
mountaintop,
as the white wall of fog
that obscures the river
like the white wall of silence
between us.

III

The burnt orange maple
yesterday was green.
Winter is coming.
Like you, the birds, too,
are leaving.

IV

Early evening hush,
dark mountain
against the still-bright sky,
silhouette of trees.
Nothing endures. Even the river
empties itself into the sea.

V.

The sun slips below the earth,
the world falls away.
I press my hand in yours
waiting—hope
is the thing that dies last.

AND STILLNESS COMES OVER THE LAND

Like water rising
the tide coming in

the darkness seeps into all the secret spaces

and the silence

which flows all day beneath the chatter
like an underground spring

breaks through

spills out
over grass and shrubs and trees
consumes the evening cries of frog and cicada

until darkness and silence are one.

AT THE EDGE OF THE LAND

This morning the beach
at the edge of the land
is strewn with mullet
as far as the horizon
in either direction, huge
mullet washed up by the tide,
some mere skeletons
picked clean, some still
intact, their mullet eyes
staring toward the sky
black with buzzards
circling, stalking,
picking at the carcasses—
and the stench of rotting flesh.

All morning we walked
across this barrier island
following the dusty road
from bay to gulf, scrub
palmettos and sawgrass
marking our way, the promise
of white sand and clear
blue water beyond the dunes,

instead it seemed
we had come upon a vision
of the end-time, that we two
were the only witnesses
that the world would end
not in fire or in ice,
but in decay, death-birds
devouring the remains.

ABOUT THE POET

Dorothy Howe Brooks writes poetry and fiction. Her work has appeared in numerous literary journals, including *Hampden-Sydney Poetry Review, Poem, Louisiana Literature,* and *Iron Horse Literary Review.* Her second chapbook, <u>Interstices</u>, was published by Finishing Line Press in 2009. She lives with her husband in Southwest Florida where they enjoy sailing in the coastal waters of the Gulf.